From Sheep to Sweater

by Ellen Tarlow

Credits appear on the inside front cover, which constitutes an extension of this copyright page.

Copyright © 2004 by Scholastic Inc.
All rights reserved. Published by Scholastic Inc.
Printed in the U.S.A.

ISBN 0-439-69706-9

SCHOLASTIC and associated logos and designs are trademarks and/or registered trademarks of Scholastic Inc.

6 7 8 9 10   23   12 11 10 09

SCHOLASTIC INC.

New York Toronto London Auckland Sydney
Mexico City New Delhi Hong Kong Buenos Aires

Here is the sheep.

Here is the wool.

Here is the yarn.

Here are the needles.

Here is the store.

Here is my sweater!